I Wonder Why

Lemons Taste Sour

and Other Questions About Senses

Deborah Chancellor

KINGFISHER

KINGFISHER

First published 2007 by Kingfisher
an imprint of Macmillan Children's Books
a division of Macmillan Publishers Ltd
The Macmillan Building,
20 New Wharf Road,
London N1 9RR
Basingstoke and Oxford
Associated companies throughout the world
www.panmacmillan.com

Consultant: David Burnie

ISBN 978-0-7534-1442-2

9 8 7 6 5 4 3
3TR/0510/SHENS/WKT/115MA

A CIP catalogue record for this book is available from the British Library.

Printed in China

Illustrations: Martn Camm 8–9, 12, 15, 16–17, 120-21, 23br, 28, 29br; Roger Stewart 4–5, 16–7, 9tr, 9br, 10–11, 13, 14, 16bl, 17br, 18–19, 21br 22, 23tr, 30–31. Peter Wilks (SGS) all cartoons.

CONTENTS

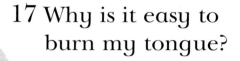

How do I know what's going on?

You have five different senses, which are sight, hearing, touch, smell and taste. Each one of your senses is very important. Together, your senses tell you what you're eating, listening to, feeling, looking at and touching.

● Your senses help you understand the world around you. They warn you of danger, but also help you to enjoy things, like music.

● Some people say they can 'feel' something happening, even though they can't see, hear, smell, taste or touch it. They call this feeling their 'sixth sense'.

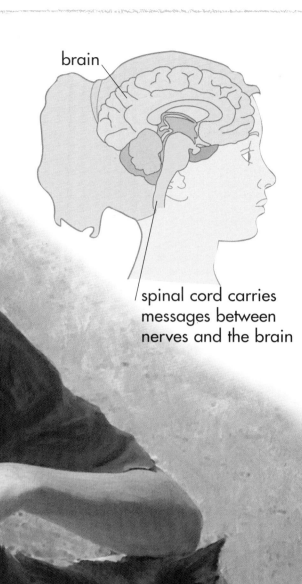

brain

spinal cord carries
messages between
nerves and the brain

Can senses get on my nerves?

Your senses cannot work without your
brain. Your eyes, ears, nose, tongue
and skin send messages to your brain
through your body's nervous system.
Your brain then tells you how to react.

Why are polar bears so sniffy?

Animals have amazing senses.
For example, a polar bear can
smell prey 20 kilometres away.
That means it will have to run half
a marathon to catch its next meal!

Why is my tongue bumpy?

Your tongue is covered with small bumps, called taste buds. When you take a mouthful of food, your taste buds send a message to your brain. This helps you identify the taste and decide if you like it. Most people like sweet things, like candyfloss.

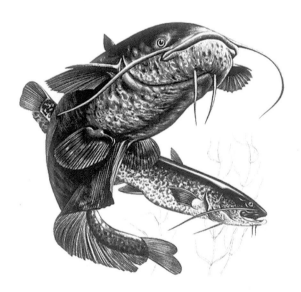

Why is a catfish like a tongue?

Catfish have taste buds all over their bodies, even on their long, whiskery barbels. They help them find food in the muddy, murky water in which they live.

● Blowflies taste with their feet! Their feet are covered with special hairs that taste the food when they land on it. If they don't like the flavour, they just buzz off.

Do girls taste better than boys?

Most people have about 10,000 taste buds inside their mouths. If you are a girl, you have more taste buds than most boys. Your taste buds are mainly on your tongue, but some are on the roof of your mouth.

● Most vegetables, such as spinach, have a bitter taste. Many children do not like this taste, but these vegetables are very good and healthy to eat.

How fussy is a koala?

The koala is the world's most picky eater. It will eat only eucalyptus leaves, and spends most of its day searching for just the right sort. Most other animals, including people, eat a lot of different things.

● Your sense of taste stops you eating things that could make you ill. Rotten apples taste bad, so you want to spit them out before you swallow them.

● The monarch butterfly is the sweet tooth champion of the animal world. It is over 1,000 times more sensitive to sweet flavours than you are!

How do I taste with my nose?

Your sense of smell is linked to your sense of taste. When you have a cold, your nose gets blocked, and you can't smell things very easily. This means you can't taste your food until you get better.

● Thousands of years ago, sweet foods, such as honey, were hard to find. Whenever our ancestors found something sweet, they ate it straight away. They developed a sweet tooth, which many of us still have today.

Why do lemons taste sour?

Lemons contain citric acid, which tastes sour. You pick up this flavour along the sides of your tongue. The lemon taste is so strong, you can tell if one drop has been mixed with 50,000 drops of water!

Which dogs sniff for trouble?

A dog's sense of smell can be up to a million times more sensitive than a human's. This is why the police and customs officers train dogs to sniff out and find hidden drugs and explosives. Police also use dogs to help find missing people.

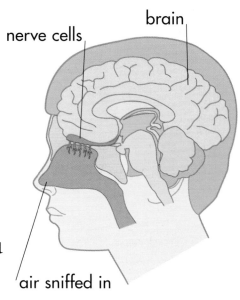

• When people are scared, their sweat contains a special chemical. This could be why dogs and horses can smell if someone is frightened. This is bad news for cowardly cowboys!

How does my brain smell?

When you sniff, air moves around inside your nose. Nerve cells recognize the smells and send signals to your brain, which tells you what you are smelling.

brain

nerve cells

air sniffed in

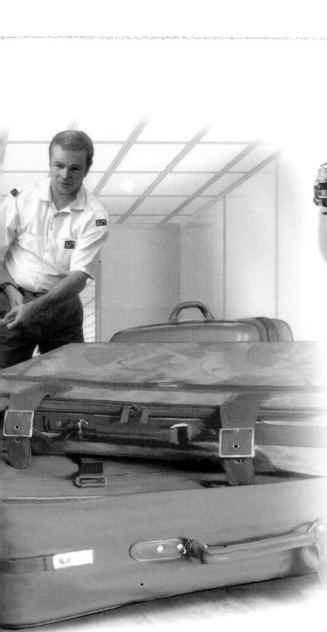

How do I escape bad smells?

Smells tell you if things are good or bad. They can warn you of danger, such as poisonous gases in the air. You can then move away from the smell before it makes you ill.

● Smells trigger the emotional part of your brain and remind you of good or bad things. Nice smells, like fresh cakes, can make you happy, while bad smells can make you cross.

● Animals use smells to mark territories, warn off predators or to attract a mate. Some male moths can smell a female over three kilometres away. It would take you about half an hour to walk that far.

Why does a skunk stink?

The skunk is the world's smelliest animal. If it is threatened by a predator, such as a bear, the skunk sprays a stinking, sticky fluid at its attacker's eyes. The liquid smells so bad, it can make the attacker sick, letting the skunk escape.

● Mosquitoes are attracted to humans by their smell. They particularly like the scent of hot, sweaty feet!

Do I smell more than my mum?

When you are young, your sense of smell is at its best. You can tell the difference between 4,000 to 10,000 smells. As you get older, you detect fewer smells. So yes, you can smell more than your mum!

● Some smells bring back memories. The smell of popcorn can make you think of your favourite film. This is because your sense of smell is linked to the bit of your brain that deals with emotions.

What's that smell?

You react quickly to smells – some are nice, but others are disgusting! There are four main kinds of smell: fragrant (like roses), fresh (like a pine forest), spicy (like cinnamon) and putrid (like rotten eggs).

When is it good to feel the heat?

You have millions of touch receptors just under your skin. They send signals to your brain, which tells you what to do next. For example, your brain tells you to move away from a fire before it burns you.

● You don't have any nerves in your hair and fingernails, so it doesn't hurt when you have them cut.

How does a ladybird tickle my finger?

Your fingertips are the most sensitive part of your body. You have about 100 touch receptors in each fingertip. This means you can feel a tickle when a ladybird moves, even if it shifts only a thousandth of a millimetre.

● When you first get dressed, you can 'feel' your clothes. Your touch receptors quickly get used to the feel of your clothes, and stop working. This is why you may forget to take off your socks before you get in the bath!

Which mole uses a star to find food?

Some animals rely on their sense of touch. The star-nosed mole can't see very well, but it uses its sense of touch to find food. It has 100,000 nerve fibres between its nose and its brain. This is almost six times more than you have in your hand.

How cool are a dog's pants?

Like many animals, a dog pants to keep cool. It may also move into the shade or splash about in some water to escape the heat.

● The desert iguana must lay her eggs when the sand is at the right temperature, or they won't hatch. This clever lizard can tell how hot the sand is, to within less than one degree centigrade.

Why do I chatter when I'm cold?

When you're cold, your muscles contract quickly to try to warm you up. We call this shivering. Your teeth chatter as the muscles in your jaw move.

● The woodland frog lives in the Arctic, where temperatures drop way below freezing. This hardy animal can survive being frozen solid!

Why is it easy to burn my tongue?

Your tongue is very sensitive to touch, but not so good at telling how warm or cold food is. If you eat something very hot, your tongue may get burned before you feel the heat.

Why does pain mean stop?

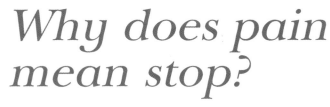

Pain is a warning to your body. Usually, if you feel pain, you need to stop doing something, or move away from something that is hurting you. When you twist your ankle, the pain warns you to stop before you hurt yourself even more.

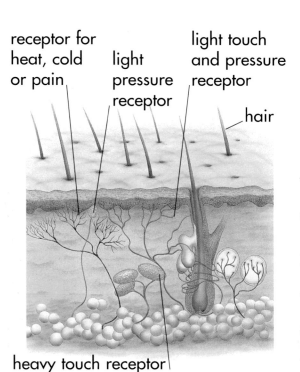

receptor for heat, cold or pain

light pressure receptor

light touch and pressure receptor

hair

heavy touch receptor

Why am I quick to feel pain?

Your sense of pain works very fast. This is because you have more pain receptors under your skin than any other kind of touch receptor. Every square centimetre of your skin packs in about 200 pain receptors.

● If you touch something sharp, like a cactus, your brain reacts so quickly that you pull away from what's hurting you, sometimes before you've even noticed.

When does ice cream hurt?

When something cold touches the roof of your mouth, it triggers a headache. Nerves feel the cold and widen blood vessels to try to warm up the brain. Luckily, the pain lasts only about 30 seconds.

19

Can dolphins make long-distance calls?

Sound travels under water, just like it does through air. Dolphins can communicate with each other over very long distances under the sea. Their sense of hearing is much better than yours.

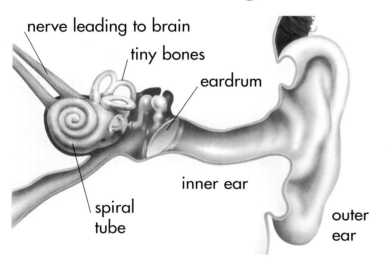

nerve leading to brain

tiny bones

eardrum

inner ear

spiral tube

outer ear

Which drum helps me hear?

You've got a drum inside each ear! A thin piece of skin, called an eardrum, wobbles when you hear a sound. The vibrations are carried through tiny bones to a spiral tube. Your brain picks up messages from the tube so you can recognize the sound.

● Children have more sensitive hearing than adults. This is why you can hear many more sounds than your grandparents.

• Snakes do not have ears, but they can hear. They pick up vibrations with their scales, muscles and bones. Inside their head, an inner ear hears the sounds.

Are two ears better than one?

You have two ears so that you can work out where a sound is coming from. A sound reaches each of your ears at a slightly different time. This helps you know whether the sound is coming from the right or the left.

How do my ears stop me from falling?

Your ears are not just listening machines. You can keep your balance thanks to what goes on inside your inner ear. Gymnasts have very good balance, and can perform exercises on a beam.

● When you are in a car, your senses can get confused. Your eyes focus on something still inside the car, but your inner ear detects that you are moving. This can make you feel horribly sick.

● An elephant's big ears are very useful on a hot day. They flap like fans, to cool the animal down.

What liquid makes me feel dizzy?

When you spin around, liquid in your inner ear spins around as well. When you stop moving, it takes a while for the liquid to stop moving too. This is why you feel dizzy for a while.

● If you climb a mountain or go up high in an aeroplane, the air pressure changes. This affects your eardrums and makes your ears pop.

Which animal is batty about echoes?

Bats have the best hearing of any land animal. A bat makes high-pitched sounds, which hit its prey and then bounce back. From this echo, the bat can work out how big the prey is, how fast it is moving and where it actually is.

Is sound speedy?

Sound travels through the air at about 1,225 kilometres per hour. Light travels much faster, so sometimes you see things before you hear them. If you watch a space shuttle launch from far away, you will see the blast before you hear the noise.

• If you blow on a dog whistle, dogs will hear the sound, but you won't. This is because the whistle has a very high frequency, which you can't hear.

• Some singers can shatter glass. If they hit exactly the right note to make the glass vibrate, then increase the volume, the glass will wobble so much that it breaks.

How loud is a whale's whistle?

The blue whale makes a whistling sound. This amazing noise measures up to 188 decibels, which is as loud as a space rocket launch!

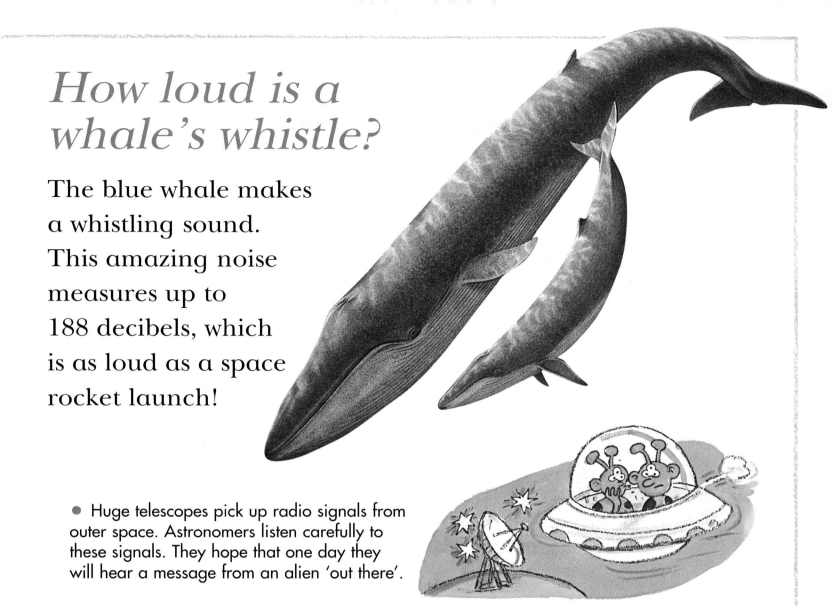

● Huge telescopes pick up radio signals from outer space. Astronomers listen carefully to these signals. They hope that one day they will hear a message from an alien 'out there'.

Which bells measure sound?

Sounds are measured in 'decibels'. A very quiet sound, like a whisper, is just 20 decibels. A jet plane taking off is about 140 decibels. The loudest sound ever heard was a volcano erupting. But be careful. If you listen to very loud sounds for too long, you will damage your ears and your hearing.

Which bird is eagle-eyed?

Eagles have incredible eye-sight. They can see a mouse move from over a kilometre away. At the back of the bird's eye, there are a million light receptor cells per millimetre. This is five times more than you have at the back of your eye.

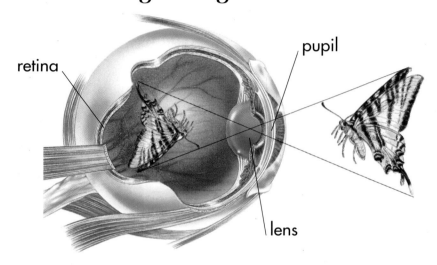

retina

pupil

lens

When is the world topsy-turvy?

When you look at an object, rays of light bounce off it and enter your eye through your pupil. These rays pass through a lens, forming an image on your retina. This image is upside-down, but your brain 'sees' it as if it were the right way up.

● The world's largest telescope is at the top of Mauna Kea, a volcano in Hawaii. The telescope is 8 storeys high, and powerful enough to see a golf ball 150 kilometres away!

● When babies are born, they gradually learn the difference between up and down. What they see is out of focus to begin with, but it is not upside down!

Which pupils grow in the dark?

You need light to see things properly. In the dark, your pupils get bigger, to let in the small amount of light that there is.

pupil becomes smaller in bright light

pupil grows larger in the dark

Can we be blinded by colour?

A rainbow shows seven different colours, but you should be able to tell the difference between about 8 million colours. But some people are colour blind, which means they can't tell the difference between some colours, especially red and green.

Why do cats' eyes glow in the dark?

At the back of a cat's eye, behind the retina, is a thin tissue that reflects light and helps the cat see better. Cats open their eyes wide in the dark, and their eyes reflect whatever small amount of light there is.

● The pygmy tarsier may be tiny, but its eyes are huge compared to its body. If your eyes were this large compared to your size, they would be as big as grapefruits!

● An ostrich's eyes are bigger than its brain!

Why is a dog's life grey?

Dogs don't have the special cells at the back of their eyes that detect colour. They see the world as shades of grey.

Why do glasses help you focus?

If you are short-sighted, you can't see things far away. If you are long-sighted, you can't see things nearby. People are long- or short-sighted because the lenses in their eyes are not quite the right shape. A pair of extra 'lenses', either glasses or contact lenses, help them see much better.

• You blink every two to ten seconds, and each blink takes about 0.3 seconds. This means that you spend about 30 minutes every day with your eyes shut, so watch out when you're walking!

Why are bright lights blinding?

Looking at very bright lights damages the light-sensitive cells at the back of your eyes. You must never look directly at the sun, not even through sunglasses. It may make you go blind.

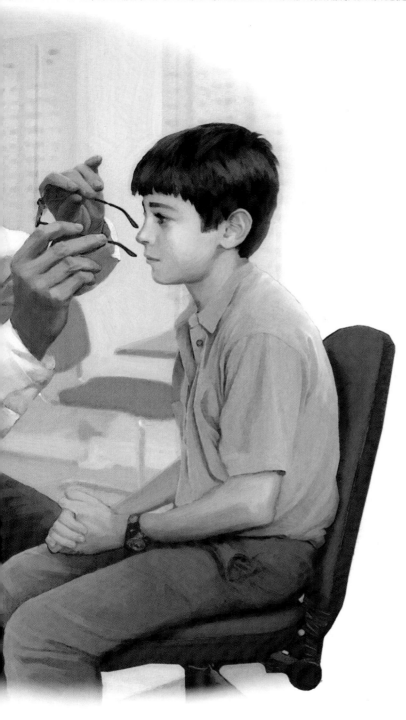

How are eyebrows like a sweatband?

Your eyebrows stop sweat from running into your eyes. You couldn't do without your eyelashes either. They keep your eyes clean and protect them from bright light.

● Crying is very good for you, because it keeps your eyes healthy. The salt water in your tears cleans your eyes and keeps them moist. Chefs who chop onions must have very healthy eyes.

● Snakes do not have eyelids, so they never shut their eyes. This means they sleep with their eyes open!

Index